WONDER VERSE

Words Of Young Hearts

First published in Great Britain in 2025 by:

YoungWriters Est. 1991

Young Writers
Remus House
Coltsfoot Drive
Peterborough
PE2 9BF
Telephone: 01733 890066
Website: www.youngwriters.co.uk

All Rights Reserved
Book Design by Neila Cepulionyte
© Copyright Contributors 2025
Softback ISBN 978-1-83685-498-2
Printed and bound in the UK by BookPrintingUK
Website: www.bookprintinguk.com
YB0641R

FOREWORD

WELCOME READER,

For Young Writers' latest competition *Wonderverse*, we asked primary school pupils to explore their creativity and write a poem on any topic that inspired them. They rose to the challenge magnificently with some going even further and writing stories too! The result is this fantastic collection of writing in a variety of styles.

Here at Young Writers our aim is to encourage creativity in children and to inspire a love of the written word, so it's great to get such an amazing response, with some absolutely fantastic pieces. This open theme of this competition allowed them to write freely about something they are interested in, which we know helps to engage kids and get them writing. Within these pages you'll find a variety of topics, from hopes, fears and dreams, to favourite things and worlds of imagination. The result is a collection of brilliant writing that showcases the creativity and writing ability of the next generation.

I'd like to congratulate all the young writers in this anthology, I hope this inspires them to continue with their creative writing.

CONTENTS

Berkeley Academy, Heston

Anahita Amiri (9)	1
Abdullahi Omar (8)	2
Arfa Tamboli (8)	3
Malaika Sandhu (7)	4
Aisha Osman (8)	5
Tarman Kour (8)	6

Craighead Primary School, Glasgow

Oscar McKechnie (11)	7
John Cochrane (11)	8
Archie Currie (11)	9
Mason Knox (11)	10
Hams Alwad (10)	11
Katie Inasirdeze (10)	12
Olly Wilson (11)	13
Kara Turner (10)	14
Harrison Day (11)	15

Cribden House School, Rawtenstall

James Quinn (10)	16
Ania Fitton (11)	17
Pippy Pilling (11)	18
Alfie Badger (10)	19
Georgie Cunningham (10)	20
William Robinson (9)	21
Jayden Durkan (10)	22

Downshall Primary School, Seven Kings

Liyaanah Rehan (9)	23

Ermington Primary School, Ermington

Louisa Wolpert-Adams (9)	24
Olivia Cole (10)	27
Lola Tillotson (10)	28
Sienna Shilpa O'Gara (10)	29
Ted Rayner	30
Isobel Tillotson (10)	32
Alice Maclellan (8)	33
Matilda Cazenave (8)	34
Nel Murray-Baker (10)	35
Jackson Giles (8)	36
Arthur Tilley (10)	37
Jessica Brewster (9)	38
Pixie Burrows (9)	39
Joesph Dalton (8)	40
Ruby Cox (9)	41
Freddie Bemister (9)	42
Arthur Cross	43
Nico R Lancaster (9)	44
Ronnie Waterton	45
Jacob Johnson (9)	46
Aarav Jetha (9)	47
Matilda W Haywood (8)	48
Neddy Ball (9)	49
Bethany Neale (9)	50

Hertford Primary School, Hollingdean

Heidi Sheehan	51
Milo Macleod (10)	52
Arlo A & Theo R H	53
Martha Corry (8)	54
Ronnie (9) & Saul	55

Adora & Martha Corry 56
Ibrahim Noori (9) & Theo Austen 57

James Cambell Primary School, Dagenham

Kansas Simmons (10) 58
Akirah Ahmed (9) 59
Gabriel Doros (10) 60
Jubilation Oluyede (9) 61
Robert Mosnianu (10) 62
Naysha Rawat (10) 63
Esther Ikeako (10) 64
Sawad Kabir (9) 65
Bendith Fatembo (7) 66
Reggie Craig (9) 67
Carina Ahwireng (9) 68
Saif Khan (10) 69

Mill Of Mains Primary School, Dundee

Beulah Ekanem (11) 70
Rhys Davidson (11) 71
Aria Anderson (12) 72
Scarlett Brown (11) 73
Cason Wilson (12) 74
Quinn Murphy (11) 75
Ethan Kinghorn (11) 76
Kaleb McIntyre (11) 77
Dylan Lamb (11) 78
Mia Sutherland (11) 79
Elise Wilkie (12) 80
Maggie-Lou Mcgarry (11) 81
Harper Nelson (12) 82
Lucas Keav (11) 83
Emily Devlin 84
Bryce Smith (11) 85

Newport School, London

Sonni Das-Munshi (10) 86
Ishmael Kneisler (11) 87
Aiza Fatima (11) 88

Nunthorpe Primary Academy, Nunthorpe

Isaac Rashid (8) 89
Thea Brown (8) 90
Elijah Kell (9) 91
Lyla Carter (8) 92
Joshua Francis (8) 93
Molly Woolams (8) 94
Tilly Hill (9) 95
Martha Rance (8) 96
Harrison Land (9) 97
Miya Wilcox (8) 98
Lucas Day (9) 99
Harry Grainger (8) 100
Kit Falcon Sanderson (9) 101
Jake Manning (9) 102
Rory Baines (9) 103
Willow Charlton (8) 104
Evan Rowcliffe (9) 105
Alfie Boalch (8) 106

Penruddock Primary School, Penruddock

Sofiia Sribna (9) 107
Ted Ware (9) 108
Daniil Sribnyi (11) 109
Bertie Williamson (8) 110
Etta Goodall (8) 111
Faith Fry (9) 112
Katie Kavanagh (9) 113

Sir Frederick Gibberd College, Harlow

Natalie Harmas (11) 114

Stoneywood Primary School, Stoneywood

Jude Bain (10) 115
Holly Mackenzie (10) 116
Nikola Kopilova (10) 117
Amelia Murray (10) 118

Archer Hippey	119
Daniel Oluwabusola (10)	120
Fatima Imran (10)	121
Aimee-Louise Edgar (10)	122

Wise Esh Winning Academy, Esh Winning

Aubree Hutchinson (10)	123
Alarna Thompson (10)	124
Logan Peart (11)	125
Ivy Hodgson (11)	126
Elsa-Mae Makepeace (10)	127
Logan Emmerson (11)	128
Jacob Jobson (10)	129
Jay Bragan (11)	130
Oliver James (11)	131
Raegan Arrowsmith (11)	132
Lillie Davy (10)	133
Ella-Jane Walker (11)	134
Lexi Leigh Kirby (11)	135
Sofia Graham (10)	136
Jack McAngus (11)	137
Olivia Wayper (11)	138
Skye Heath (10)	139
Jesse Brown (10)	140
Evie Kirkup (10)	141
Hollie Lyon (10)	142
Lucas Hodgson (11)	143
Teddy Peveller (10)	144

THE POEMS AND STORIES

The Wonder Of A Garden

With every breath you take,
Here's a crystal blue lake.
Smell the wonder of each flower,
You will notice none are sour.

Fill me with the wonder,
Of true wildlife, let me see,
Smell, hear and touch.
The music and movement of such a place.

As the greenery fades away,
Here comes the next day,
Do not tease,
After all, they are only nectar bees.

Fill me with the wonder,
Of true and attractive wildlife.
Let me see, smell, hear and touch,
The music, the movement of such a place.

After all, we do have
The responsibility to look after
The nature and wildlife around us.

Anahita Amiri (9)
Berkeley Academy, Heston

The Mad Metal Monster

The Metal Monster, covered in rust
Makes people look at him in disgust.
His arms, made out of metal,
Can shoot out heat like the temperature of a kettle.
His enormous hands
Are the size of great lands.
The iron giant's legs
Can cling onto anything, like pegs.
When he steps,
His feet make a loud beat.
His face is as big as a hidden base,
Yet the material is like a phone case.
The Metal Monster's black eyes
Are as dark as cursed treasure,
Whoever looks at it meets their demise.

Abdullahi Omar (8)
Berkeley Academy, Heston

Eid

Eid is fun.
Eid is a celebration.
Eid is when lots of people
Go to people's houses
Or spend time with their families.

Eid is amazing.
Whenever you meet someone,
Like your grandparents,
You always say, "Eid Mubarak!"

Before Eid, there is Ramadan.
Ramadan is for one month,
Eid is for only one day.
We pray and tell God
All the bad deeds we've done.

We all get presents.
Whenever it's Eid,
I will wish you an 'Eid Mubarak!'

Arfa Tamboli (8)
Berkeley Academy, Heston

Mental Health Matters

I don't have to feel bad
When I am sad
I just went to my dad
When I am mad
My dad asked me what's on my mind
I asked, "Why is it hard for people to be kind?"
He said, "Everyone is different!"
Yes, but they can still be considerate
When I grow, I will show
That we can all be different
But yet to be considered
Let's stop the chatter
As mental health matters.

Malaika Sandhu (7)
Berkeley Academy, Heston

Seasons

October brings the leaves
And it's not heaves
Then the wind blows
And it's really slow
The trees are waving
And also swaying.

Welcome to January and Happy New Year
It's time for a new start, time for a new year.

Here comes April with all the flowers
Then the bees come with all their powers.

In July you can play in the sun
You can have a lot of fun.

Aisha Osman (8)
Berkeley Academy, Heston

Little Butterfly

Above you little butterfly the clouds running by,
Beside you little butterfly the wind rushing by,
Underneath you little butterfly the greenery jumping by.

As you go by, the flowers dance in happiness,
As you go by, the trees move with joy,
As you go by, the grass waves in great spirit,
As you go by, the sun smiles.

At last, the little butterfly said bye-bye.

Tarman Kour (8)
Berkeley Academy, Heston

Biscuits

Go to sleep, as they said,
Chocolate biscuits in my head.

"What to do?" I smell their scent,
Waiting for chocolate biscuits to be in my bed.

Slowly but surely, I walk down the stairs,
Oops, I stand on the cat's tail.

Squeal after squeal, the cat moans,
My parents get up to give me a roar!

Back to bed, I shimmy and wait,
"Oh, what can I do?" Only wait.

But the biscuits are still not in my mouth,
I give up for another day,
But the biscuits still stay in their place.

Oscar McKechnie (11)
Craighead Primary School, Glasgow

Dark Deceptions

D on't play at night.
A n amazing game.
R eally scary.
K ids would easily get scared if they play.

D ifficult
E very chapter gets more difficult.
C reepy, very creepy.
E very monster is scary.
P eople get scared playing the game.
T he game has four chapters with a fifth on the way.
I t's fun to play.
O ne of my favourite games to play.
N ot an easy game.
S o many monsters, so many levels.

John Cochrane (11)
Craighead Primary School, Glasgow

Exotic Food

E xotic, soft, juicy
X tra sauce
O iled pan-seared steak
T rout cooked on the grill
I ce cream melts slowly
C reamy mashed potato

F lavoured food
O lives, meat and cheese
O vercooked sometimes
D elicious!

Archie Currie (11)
Craighead Primary School, Glasgow

Untitled

The gun barrel staring back at me,
Shooting as fast as an aeroplane.

The mighty vault door,
Thicker than a concrete wall.

Fighting, one way out, almost felt impossible,
Almost as hard as lifting a car.

Living in luxury with £100 million in my pocket.

Mason Knox (11)
Craighead Primary School, Glasgow

Growing Up

The girl is mad,
The girl feels bad,
The girl is so sad.

I think she's grown.

Now she's moaning,
All her emotions are growing.

What's bad about growing?

Now she's throwing,
But that's just growing.

Hams Alwad (10)
Craighead Primary School, Glasgow

Gymnastics...

Feels like a soft pillow.
Smells like a sweaty person who just came back from a run.
Looks like the perfect place.
Sounds like feet clapping on the ground.

Katie Inasirdeze (10)
Craighead Primary School, Glasgow

Go Karting

Adrenaline rush
Speeding past
Body controlling
Sharp decisions
Mood thrilling
Tyres burning
Last... Man... Standing!

Olly Wilson (11)
Craighead Primary School, Glasgow

The Sea

The sand crawling through my feet,
As I eat another treat.
As I sit and stare in my chair,
Watching the waves wander.

Kara Turner (10)
Craighead Primary School, Glasgow

Crystals

A haiku

Blue or red or green,
Textures, types, all different,
Crystals are awesome!

Harrison Day (11)
Craighead Primary School, Glasgow

Football

F ields of grass; when the players come in, the pitch gets muddy
O ut and about, the team players are scoring
O verwatched by their fans who are cheering
T ea and coffee in their hands
B all getting kicked around, and the players scoring
A ll the time losing games but we don't mind
L ong ball shots, we're trying to score
L ong corner shots, we're trying to get them in.

James Quinn (10)
Cribden House School, Rawtenstall

Unicorns

U nique and sparkly as glitter,
N ever boring because it's as pretty as a star,
I ncredibly beautiful, elegant and sweet,
C hildren love them, they make them smile,
O ver the rainbow they go,
R acing on rainbows they go,
N avigating through the stars,
S weet as can be.

Ania Fitton (11)
Cribden House School, Rawtenstall

Our Place

This place is different from the others.
In this place, we feel like brothers.
Autism is what most of us have.
Autism is what makes me mad.
This is the best place for us.
This is where we play in the mud.
This is where children bounce.
This is our school, Cribden House.

Pippy Pilling (11)
Cribden House School, Rawtenstall

All About My Cat

W onderful little cat,
H e always begs for food,
I s always wanting to play,
P urrs like an engine,
S ometimes he explores the garden,
Y ou will know when he is angry.

Alfie Badger (10)
Cribden House School, Rawtenstall

Jane Moore

Kind person
Nice woman
Treat journalist
Phenomenal presenter
Laugh maker
Best dressed
Truth teller.

Georgie Cunningham (10)
Cribden House School, Rawtenstall

Untitled

Flag waving
Car revving
Tyres smoking
Engines squeak
Trails blowing
My hobby
Racecar.

William Robinson (9)
Cribden House School, Rawtenstall

Minecraft

It has horns
It has an upside-down mouth
It has a ribcage
It has a heart and is made out of block.

Jayden Durkan (10)
Cribden House School, Rawtenstall

Space

I have never been to space,
But I'm still okay,
I might go in May,
But then I still have to stay.

I'm still a bit worried,
Because my whole family's going,
But I just remembered,
I'm still going to be okay,
Because the moon is showing.

Liyaanah Rehan (9)
Downshall Primary School, Seven Kings

Once Upon A Time

Once upon a time
In a nursery rhyme
Were Mr and Mrs Splat
Who lived in a council flat
With their big dog and little cat

They had two babies
Called Tom and Davies
And danced with joy
Even though their dog had rabies

They sold their dog
And bought another called Mog
Who ate a poisonous frog
Named Gregory

Poor old Mog
Got thrown in a bog
And replaced by another dog named
Silly old Bob

Bob ate the cat
Who ate the bat
Who ate the rat
That sat on the carpet

Ugly fat Bob
Joined an
Ugly fat mob
And took away Tom to eat

Davies cried, "No!"
And ate his big toe
Then threw up a million times

Away from home
He rode on a gnome
And landed in a beehive
Which was quite a ride

When he got to the kidnapper's house
He saw Tom was now a mouse
He ate Tom up
And out he popped
As a louse

The louse became a boy
And they sailed away
Until one of them cried
"Land Ahoy!"

Once upon a time
In a nursery rhyme

Were Mr and Mrs Splat
Who lived in a council flat
With their little babies
Tom and Davies.

Louisa Wolpert-Adams (9)
Ermington Primary School, Ermington

The Story Of My Life

T he house is packed with fun and cheer,
H ere I stand all tall and clear,
E nough is enough when the parents say no!

S ilence, silence is never near,
T he best it could be, but life is never clear,
O h, how I love horses and friends,
R ight about the craziness, but never about the tiredness,
Y et, the world is mind-blowing.

O n the challenging side of things, do not stop rowing,
F or there will be one chance for the showing,

M y life is full of obstacles like a roller coaster,
Y et I've never given up, but I'm not a boaster.

L ife is full of fun, laughter, tears and joy,
I f you are fun, you will need a toy,
F or all the readers out there, keep going and never give up,
E nd is coming near, so now I must go!

Olivia Cole (10)
Ermington Primary School, Ermington

Meadows Of Feelings

M esmerising flowers as colourful as can be
E nchanting woods surround me
A nts carry leaves and build outstanding towers
D ogs leaping through all the lovely flowers
O h, how the sun reflects on the lake
W onderful colours build up to make a cake.

O h yes, we cannot forget
F eelings are here to help us reset.

F orever and ever, they are here
E motions can fill our eyes with tears
E ven the strongest person feels down
L et them in, you are not a clown
I n your mind, it is hard to find your way
N ever give up and you will not stray
G o let them in, you cannot throw them in the bin
S o yes, it's okay to feel that way.

Lola Tillotson (10)
Ermington Primary School, Ermington

Car Journey

"Are we nearly there yet?"
Asked the children from the back.
"No," I said, about to make a threat.

"I want to watch TV," one said.
"I want to play a game."
"I want to play football."
"This is soooooo lame!"

My husband fell asleep.
Now I was left alone.
The car went *beep*.
It was just me and the children, now.

"Look out the window," I said.
"Look at the mountains and valleys."
"Nope!" they said. "I'd rather go to bed!"
I was now getting bored.
"Are we nearly there yet?"
They just got ignored!

Sienna Shilpa O'Gara (10)
Ermington Primary School, Ermington

The Tiger

Thy tiger
I see you there
Standing surreal
In the forests of the night
I see your eyes
Filled with might

Your body
It's symmetrical with no doubt
Thy must not slay this creature

I see your jaws
Fearsome beast
You crave my blood
So I must be careful

Thy fiery orange
Thy evil black
Why we kill them
Thy will never know

The way thy prowl
The way thy drink
The way thy growl

What are you hiding
Unblinking creature

So thy tiger
I see you there
Standing surreal
In the forests of the night
I see your eyes
Filled with might

Do not slay
This fearful symmetry.

Ted Rayner
Ermington Primary School, Ermington

Baking A Poem

Baking a poem,
What should I make?
An ice cream cone with a chocolate flake?
It smells so good,
What should I do?
I'll add something new.

I'll add an acrostic,
Oh, I think I've lost it,
Not again, I'll get the blame.

Now I'll put the ice cream in the freezer,
Because it's always a pleaser.
My tummy rumbles while I wait,
I feel so humble, I can't wait.

Soon it's ready,
Nice and steady as I take it out.
I sprinkle some simile right on top,
It smells so good I can't stop.

Then I eat it,
And,
You just can't beat it.

Isobel Tillotson (10)
Ermington Primary School, Ermington

Puppies

Puppies with their mummy,
Their mummy is called Honey,
Puppies are very funny,
Time for food to go in their tummy,
They're getting new collars,
Woof lots of money,

Black, brown, gold and all,
Careful puppies try not to fall,
If you want a puppy then come and call,
Just to let you know they like to run around the hall,
Though they may be active they are only small,

When it's bedtime,
Don't cross the line,
"Oi" that squeaky toy is mine,

One's called Stella,
One's name is Ella,
Her name is Bella.

Alice Maclellan (8)
Ermington Primary School, Ermington

Kittens

The cute little kittens on the bed
Sometimes they climb on my head
They have collars made of lead

Ginger, black, red and all
Be careful not to fall
Are the vets going to call?

When is bedtime?
That mouse is mine
Don't cross the line!

The kittens are almost cats
They love sitting on mats
They are very, very cute
And they're never ever on mute!

Matilda Cazenave (8)
Ermington Primary School, Ermington

Me And My Mind Of Poems

Me and my mind
Can't think of a poem
What should I do
Should I write about a shoe
Should it say *Boo!*

Me and my mind can't think of a rhyme
Should I do 'the cat sat on the mat'
And I think that's that.

Why can't me and my mind
Think of a poem or a rhyme?
Wait, I thought of one already!

Nel Murray-Baker (10)
Ermington Primary School, Ermington

Boat, Goat, Bird!

I went on the river on my boat
until I got to a waterfall,
My boat turned into a goat,
So the goat swam and swam
until it couldn't swim again,
So it turned into a bird,
So we flew over the river
until the bird's wings got wet,
So it fell down to the river
and it disappeared,
So I got wet!

Jackson Giles (8)
Ermington Primary School, Ermington

Mav

Mav the cat got in a plane
He flew to Spain
Where it started to rain
He was washed down the drain.

He landed on a mat
And broke his bat
With a big splat
He made friends with a rat.

The rat built a plane
It was made from a crane
He flew back from Spain
In the plane.

Arthur Tilley (10)
Ermington Primary School, Ermington

My Neighbour's Dog

My neighbour's dog, Rufus, loves to play with Mog the cat,
My neighbour's dog, Rufus, barks at the bark on a tree,
My neighbour's dog, Rufus, plays with a horse that goes, "Neigh."
"Finally, Rufus is asleep!" said Mog. "Now I can go out and play!"

Jessica Brewster (9)
Ermington Primary School, Ermington

Mirror, Mirror

Mirror, mirror, look at me,
I see my reflection,
What do you see?
Do you see a little tiny bee?
Do you see someone standing free?
Do you see a tall girl?
Do you see someone twirl?
What can you find?
Can you find someone kind?
Mirror, mirror, look at me.

Pixie Burrows (9)
Ermington Primary School, Ermington

Zoo Monkeys

Z ipping all over
O ooing
O ver and over

M onkeys are cheeky
O ooing again
N ibbling each other's fleas
K nocking each other's knees
E verywhere
Y apping like Year 4 and 5.

Joesph Dalton (8)
Ermington Primary School, Ermington

Tigger

T igger springs around from here and there
I ndestructible without a care
G reat, happy, amazing and funny
G obbles Pooh's honey in his tummy
E ager to pounce, easy to love
R egularly chaotic but loves a hug.

Ruby Cox (9)
Ermington Primary School, Ermington

The Wonderverse

The Wonderverse is very good,
You can write about anything
And you should.

You can write about football or rugby
Even about a boy called Cubby!

You can follow my creation
But in your own imagination!

Freddie Bemister (9)
Ermington Primary School, Ermington

Kittens

K ittens playing
I n the bedding
T aking each other's toys
T eaching themselves
E very great
N ation of
S cratching the curtains.

Arthur Cross
Ermington Primary School, Ermington

Sports

Some you run
Some you hit a ball
Some you get muddy
But I like them all
When you get on the pitch
With a team or on your own
All you think about
Is go big or go home.

Nico R Lancaster (9)
Ermington Primary School, Ermington

Zeus

He is as fluffy as a cloud
Eyes as blue as the sky
He is as calm as a koala
As soon as he arrived
My family was complete
Zeus means the world to me
And he always will.

Ronnie Waterton
Ermington Primary School, Ermington

Jacob The Goon

J umping around like a goon,
A cting like a buffoon,
C ausing a rumpus,
O scar lent me his compass,
B ut instead, he followed the balloon.

Jacob Johnson (9)
Ermington Primary School, Ermington

Orange

O ranges are juicy
R ipe too
A way to make orange juice
N amed after the colour orange
G rows on trees
E xcellent food.

Aarav Jetha (9)
Ermington Primary School, Ermington

Fly Far

I am a red dot
I can fly
Fly far
Far from you
Flap my wings, go
I have dots
Black ones
What am I?

Answer: I'm a ladybug.

Matilda W Haywood (8)
Ermington Primary School, Ermington

Home

Home is a happy place
A place to make memories
A place to feel safe
A place to be loved
A place to love
A place to never leave
That is...
Home.

Neddy Ball (9)
Ermington Primary School, Ermington

Calm Acrostic

C ome and have peace with me,
A nd calm yourself down,
L ay down and relax,
M editating and breathing.

Bethany Neale (9)
Ermington Primary School, Ermington

Christmas

Twenty days before Christmas,
"Oh no, we forgot to get the Christmas tree."
My family always forgets the Christmas tree.

Nineteen days before Christmas,
Finally, we have the Christmas tree.

Eighteen days before Christmas,
My mum is rushing about getting presents for everyone.

Two days later.
Sixteen days before Christmas,
Sorting out presents.
Presents are coming to my house.

Eight days until Christmas.
My dad is wrapping presents.

Seven days later.
Christmas Eve, cooking in the kitchen.
Kids are jumping about.

Christmas Day,
Everyone is looking in their stockings.

Heidi Sheehan
Hertford Primary School, Hollingdean

Seasons

Spring, the flowers thrive,
The air is fresh,
And I'm cooking some animal flesh,
The grass is green,
Oh, I love what I've seen,
Summer, the sun is hot,
I love this season a lot.
Autumn, I love Halloween,
I get a sweet,
And there are people in costumes
Walking down my street,
Winter, snow is falling,
And Santa is in my chimney, crawling.

Milo Macleod (10)
Hertford Primary School, Hollingdean

Counting Nature

Counting slugs
Counting snails
Counting trees, leaves, bees and peas?
Finding cobwebs
Finding spiders
Finding bugs of all sizes
One cobweb
Two slugs
Three snails
Four bugs
Five
Six
Seven spiders
Eight woodlice
Nine worms
Goodbye
Hang on, we haven't reached ten!
Ten beetles
Goodbye again!

Arlo A & Theo R H
Hertford Primary School, Hollingdean

Dogs

Dogs can be fluffy,
Dogs are cute,
Dogs can be a joy in your life,
Dogs are playful,
Dogs can be interesting,
Dogs are happy,
Dogs can be part of the family.

Dogs are soft,
Dogs can be big,
Dogs are clever,
Dogs can be small,
Dogs are amazing.
I wish I had a dog.

Martha Corry (8)
Hertford Primary School, Hollingdean

Dragons

D ragons are cool!
R aging, rampaging dragons!
A mazing creatures, they are!
G oing to sleep - they are so lazy!
O ngoing fires, they make so many!
N ot quitting creatures, they are!
S ometimes water, sometimes fire. There are so many!

Ronnie (9) & Saul
Hertford Primary School, Hollingdean

Nature

Wind,
Air whistling in the breeze,
Animals,
Creatures hibernating for winter,
Plants,
Trees swaying in the wind,
Magic,
Mythical creatures all around,
Adventurers.

Adora & Martha Corry
Hertford Primary School, Hollingdean

Goodbye Earth

Extra destructive
Abnormal life, destruction
Regular humans disappear
Goodbye Earth
Things now demolished
All existence discouraged.

Ibrahim Noori (9) & Theo Austen
Hertford Primary School, Hollingdean

Seasons

S pring is the start of a fantastic new year,
P roves that summer is coming ahead quick,
R ight time of year to start getting ready for summer,
I n spring it is still cold but hot too,
N othing beats a pile of flowers,
G o have fun in the flowers,

S ummer is the time of year to get money and buy ice cream,
U nder your clothes you are hot,
M y point is to get ice cream every day,
M ake sure you read lots,
E verything you do, make sure you have fun,
R ight or wrong, always have fun no matter what happens,

A utumn is the time of year you get to look for conkers
U nderneath the leaves, there are thousands of conkers,
T ime goes by. Day by day, the leaves fall off
U nder their clothes, they are cold,
M y opinion is to stay home in bed,
N ow is the end of autumn, so get ready for winter.

Kansas Simmons (10)
James Cambell Primary School, Dagenham

The Big Chase

Two little friends, a bunny and a lemur,
We're playing in the field.
Along came a bear, who was hungry and fierce,
He chased and chased and chased until the bunny hit a tree.
Along with a tree, hit a beehive, as they ran and ran, the bees joined the queue.
Then a tiger came looking hungrier than ever,
They ran and hid, except the two friends,
As they weren't afraid of a silly old tiger,
They ran and ran for hours and hours.
The tiger began to stop, as it was tired from running,
As he fell to the floor, the friends went too,
Help, the bear and bees helped as well.
As they did so, they became the best of friends.

Akirah Ahmed (9)
James Cambell Primary School, Dagenham

Hot Or Cold Seasons

Spring is the season meant for flowers,
Spring season shouts, "It's time for Easter!"
Time for an Easter egg hunt, run, run, run,
Spring is now over, time for summer.

Summer is here, time to have fun,
School is over, time to travel to beaches and water parks.
Summer's over, time for autumn.

Back to school, autumn is here!
New things to learn and new goals to achieve.
Autumn is over, winter's here.

Bang! Winter has come,
Snowballs are thrown at the speed of light.
Christmas is here, time to open presents,
Time for the New Year.
New year, new me.

Gabriel Doros (10)
James Cambell Primary School, Dagenham

All About Space

Space, a canvas vast and bright,
With planets, stars, and endless light.
The sun, a blazing ball of fire,
Warms the Earth and lifts us higher.

Planets spin around its glow,
Mercury, Venus, in steady flow,
Earth, our home, with life so near,
Mars, the red world, dry and bare.

Jupiter, giant, with storm so grand,
Saturn rings like a golden band,
Uranus tilts, a sideways dance,
Neptune's wind in a mystic trance.

Pluto, distant, cold and small,
A tiny speck among them all.
The moon above, so round and bright,
Pulls the tides and guards the night.

Jubilation Oluyede (9)
James Cambell Primary School, Dagenham

Bella, My Friend

On a beautiful spring day, my parents told me to go to someone, who was going to show us something. Arriving there and entering the yard a puppy jumped into my arms. I liked her so much that I started to cry for joy. My parents, seeing how happy I was, told me it was my puppy. From that moment on, I named her Bella because she was a little girl. I took great care of her. I went to the doctor and bought her food and she became my best friend. Unfortunately, a year later, I had to leave her with my aunt because we had to move to England. I miss her a lot, but I know she is happy with my aunt and I can see her anytime on the phone.

Robert Mosnianu (10)
James Cambell Primary School, Dagenham

Harmony Of Contrasts

In a forest, a panda sits, a gentle giant,
Like a cloud of black and white,
Soft as a whisper,
Calm in the moon's glow.

The wolf prowls, a shadow in the night,
Eyes like embers, fierce as a storm,
Silent as the wind,
Swift as a fleeting thought.

Together they meet, in the twilight's hush,
The panda, a mountain of peace,
The wolf, a river of strength.

United, they are a balance of peace and power,
A harmony of contrasts,
Like the sun and the moon, sharing the sky.

Naysha Rawat (10)
James Cambell Primary School, Dagenham

Friends

F rom the day that I can remember
R eal friends stick by you like glue
I should always remember the day we met just like December
E very friend has their own quality like parents and their qualities
N ever ever leave your friend in a time of trouble or you're being a bully
D o not leave your friend or they're gonna double
S tick together forever and ever.

Esther Ikeako (10)
James Cambell Primary School, Dagenham

Summertime, Summertime!

Summertime, summertime
Let's go outside and play
Summertime, summertime
Making the most of these sunny days.

Summertime, summertime
We're glad you're here
Let's all cheer!

Summertime, summertime
Having fun
In this glorious, golden sun.

Summertime, summertime
Going to bed during the day.
That's unfair - I wanted to play!

Sawad Kabir (9)
James Cambell Primary School, Dagenham

Springtime

The chirp of the birds awakes me
Flowers grow
A river flows

A deer gallops in the distance
All joy and bright
Sun and night
Day after day!

A new baby comes to life!
A new bundle of joy
Is in our sight

Whoa! Cherry blossoms are in the cool, breezy air
The sun is in the sky, sunbeams are everywhere.

This is springtime!

Bendith Fatembo (7)
James Cambell Primary School, Dagenham

Reggie's World

R eggie likes to play football and when he grows up
E veryone will want to play with him
G etting to play football with his teammates makes him happy
G etting to play football with his friends is better than playing by himself
I want to succeed in football
E veryone will want to play football.

Reggie Craig (9)
James Cambell Primary School, Dagenham

Growing Up

Growing up, you need to eat healthy food
So you need to be hydrated and eat fruit,
Vegetables and protein.
You need to do exercise,
So you can grow well and healthy in the future.

Carina Ahwireng (9)
James Cambell Primary School, Dagenham

The Winter Sky

A haiku

In the winter sky
Snowflakes trickle from the sky.
Cold, quiet winter night.

Saif Khan (10)
James Cambell Primary School, Dagenham

Pizza

The perfect place shines in the distance.
Sometimes, I just can't resist it.
I smell the scent already.
I can somehow taste the scent I'm smelling.
Slowly, I happily march in.
And get a huge whiff of the smell I was smelling.
I take a piece up to my face.
As my heart begins to race.
I take a huge bite and...
A magical glow fogs up my sight.
My eyes begin to fill up with joy.
As I prance out of the shop and enjoy.
Sizzle, sizzle, sizzle, the noise the pizza makes.
When I took a bite, it felt like an earthquake.
When I was young, I only ate the meat.
But now, I eat the whole thing, complete.

Beulah Ekanem (11)
Mill Of Mains Primary School, Dundee

The Flower Of Scotland

S cotland is one of the best countries in the world,
C ountryside is as beautiful as a summer's day,
O f course, we have the best water compared to the world,
T he houses are like palaces,
L ush fields for days,
A nd the greatest of all-time footballers, Scott McTominay is Scottish,
N obody hates Scotland because the people are friendly,
D oke is a brilliant young footballer for Scotland.

Rhys Davidson (11)
Mill Of Mains Primary School, Dundee

Jellycats

J ellycats are as cute as puppies.
E veryone is obsessed with them.
L eaping with joy when it first arrives.
L ying with a cuddly toy.
Y ou will gain a whole collection.
C arefully take it out of the bag to see your brand-new friend.
A ccidentally made my bank account go boom.
T hank God it's payday.
S hocked at how many I own.

Aria Anderson (12)
Mill Of Mains Primary School, Dundee

Maggie-Lou Friendship

M agical as a fairy in a castle
A s pretty as a flower in a field
G reat helper, always helping me
G lamorous outfits
I love her energy; always happy
E ating bread all the time
-
L oud as a foghorn, *honk!*
O utgoing with smartness
U nderstands my problems and helps me solve them.

Scarlett Brown (11)
Mill Of Mains Primary School, Dundee

The Highlands

B eautiful hills in the Highlands
A lot of people play football
G lasgow is as beautiful as a sunrise
P eople in Scotland love dancing and singing
I rn-Bru is like magic to the tongue
P eople in Scotland are like no other
E dinburgh is the capital, it is beautiful
S cotland is full of Highlands and cities.

Cason Wilson (12)
Mill Of Mains Primary School, Dundee

About Scotland

T he beautiful Highlands
H ectic city centres filled with great people
I rn-Bru is the famous Scottish drink
S eagulls desperately swoop down to take our food
T unnock's Tea Cakes are in every granny's biscuit tin
L ovely hills and mountains stretch for miles
E veryone loves to join in the Cèilidhs.

Quinn Murphy (11)
Mill Of Mains Primary School, Dundee

Scotland

S cotland is a beautiful country
C ities are full of attractions
O minous crackling noises, crack
T owns always full of friendly people
L ush fields for miles
A lways a fun place to be
N obody hates Scotland
D undee is the sunniest city.

Ethan Kinghorn (11)
Mill Of Mains Primary School, Dundee

The Leopard

L ying on the Sahara, the sun beating down.
E very leopard hunts prey like an eagle.
O utdoor dominance.
P rowling through the day.
A nd as sneaky as a ninja!
R oar! Run and don't look back.
D ead if it catches you, beware of the leopard.

Kaleb McIntyre (11)
Mill Of Mains Primary School, Dundee

Irn-Bru

I rn Bru, the best in Scotland.
R un for your life, it's the Irn-Bru!
N o drinking Coke, drink Irn-Bru.
-
B e kind and earn yourselves a can of Irn-Bru.
R est in bed with a can of Irn-Bru.
U nder the covers is your Irn-Bru stash.

Dylan Lamb (11)
Mill Of Mains Primary School, Dundee

Spring

S unsets are as sparkly as diamonds.
P ineapples are starting to grow.
R oses as red as a ruby.
I n the sky is where birds fly as high as trees can grow.
N ature is as pretty as gold.
G rass is as green as a lime.

Mia Sutherland (11)
Mill Of Mains Primary School, Dundee

Harper

H appy as a bird, chirping in the trees
A s sassy as a poodle walking
R adiant as the sun on a summer's day
P retty as a gem, shining in the sunlight
E legant as an ice skater spinning
R are as an emerald.

Elise Wilkie (12)
Mill Of Mains Primary School, Dundee

Scarlett

S mart as a mathematician
C aring soul
A lways makes me laugh
R eally sweet like candy
L oud, like a firework cracking
E veryone likes her
T all as a giant
T alks all the time.

Maggie-Lou Mcgarry (11)
Mill Of Mains Primary School, Dundee

Untitled

E lectric as an eel, slithering in the water
L oyal as a dog to their owner
I s as pretty as the spring flowers blooming
S weet like sugar on a doughnut
E legant as a gazelle, swishing in the grass.

Harper Nelson (12)
Mill Of Mains Primary School, Dundee

Rex

A haiku

He really hates cats
He is a German Shepherd
His bark is loud. *Woof!*

Lucas Keav (11)
Mill Of Mains Primary School, Dundee

Highland Cows

A haiku

Highland cows are cute,
Running through the countryside,
Like a small puppy.

Emily Devlin
Mill Of Mains Primary School, Dundee

Dogs

A haiku

I love to pet them
They love to run at the park
They are very cute.

Bryce Smith (11)
Mill Of Mains Primary School, Dundee

A Beautiful Space

In the velvet vastness, a vengeful void,
Where stars sing softly, their songs employed,
The moon murmurs in mysterious tones,
Like silver secrets in celestial zones.

A wonderful nebulous night,
Dancing with planets in the deep dark light,
Galaxies fly with a graceful glide,
While comets collide with such pride.

The planets sung with a satisfying hum,
Booming gently like a cosmic drum,
Each orbit goes round and round,
As meteors zoom with thunderous sounds.

Shooting stars fly with a quiver,
Flying through space like shimmering silver,
Galaxies go on like a never-ending maze,
Oh, what a beautiful space!

Sonni Das-Munshi (10)
Newport School, London

Sleepless Nights

Sleepless nights come and go
Baby crying high and low
I try my best to get to sleep
And force my eyes not to peep

The clock ticks, my mind is open wide
Awaiting dreams that it may provide
The moonlight dances cold and bright
I search for calm in endless night

Staring at the ceiling, lost in thought
Thinking of lessons my teacher has taught
My mind is like an endless road
Thoughts provoking an infinite code

Sleepless nights come and go
Whispers in the dark, soft and slow
And through the night, I find my way
Waiting for dawn to break the day.

Ishmael Kneisler (11)
Newport School, London

The Bridge Of Friendship

Friendship is a sunny day.
Smiles and laughter light the way.
Hand in hand, we always stand,
Together strong, as a perfect band,

No storm can break, no wind can sway,
This bridge of ours will always stay,
For friendship's bridge, so firm, so true,
Will always link my heart to you.

Aiza Fatima (11)
Newport School, London

Aston Villa Vs Manchester City

It was a cold football match, if Aston Villa win, they will win the Championship League.

Man City kicked off. Aston Villa pressured Man City and scored by Morgan Rogers. But soon Man City scored. It was a penalty for Aston Villa. They scored. What a game. Villa were still two-one up.

Erling Haaland shoots, "But could he score? Yes, he does!"

Two-two, who will win? Man City had been awarded a penalty to turn this game around. Man City goalkeeper was taking it. It went wide. Aston Villa counterattacks them. The goalkeeper booted it and he passed it to Villa. He went for the shot and he scored it somehow. Three-two. The game started again. Man City were desperate for a goal. But the game finished, Aston Villa, three, Man City two. One side of the pitch was in celebration.

Isaac Rashid (8)
Nunthorpe Primary Academy, Nunthorpe

Nature Girls

Trees and bees love the breeze to blow the tree.
Strong girls make waves to be brave under the cave.
They went through the forest and saw trees and bees,
And cute birds under their nest.

The girls followed the leaves and the bees,
To a place they did not know,
Where did that tree and bee go?
The bee probably flew like a fairy.

The tree flicked its branches in the breeze,
And you could not even hear anything out of the girls' mouths.
The nature carried on growing through the springtime.

The next day it was summer.
And suddenly the nature girls appeared.
Now the trees were over 200 years old,
And the girls found out that they were in a coma.

Thea Brown (8)
Nunthorpe Primary Academy, Nunthorpe

Outer Space

Newton was the first to discover gravity.
In space, it does not exist, not even for me.
I'd like to discover a big black hole.
When I grow up, this would be my goal.

To get there, I would need a rocket
But I don't have enough money in my pockets.
I would need to be a billionaire
To have enough money to get up there!

I could see galaxies and Mars.
I could smell chocolate bars.
I could see the moon, the Earth and the sun
And know that I was the chosen one.

I might see asteroids, comets and constellations
And park my rocket at a space station.
But, right now, I can only dream of my space flight
As my mum kisses me goodnight.

Elijah Kell (9)
Nunthorpe Primary Academy, Nunthorpe

Hope

Once in a silent village,
Sadness invaded each house,
It seemed deserted,
But eerie people were
Silent as a mouse.
But one day their lives changed forever,
In the shadows they whispered, "What is this thing?"
So sparkly and bright, they couldn't sleep at night,
In hope the people gathered around,
Watch this,
Bang!
Confetti went everywhere,
The people started to laugh,
Smile and party all night,
That's hope, it makes people happy!

Lyla Carter (8)
Nunthorpe Primary Academy, Nunthorpe

My Dragon Friend

I have a dragon, big and bright,
With wings that shine at night.
His eyes glow green, his scales are red,
He sleeps beside my little bed.

He breathes out fire, but never burns,
And tells me when the seasons turn.
He flies me high up in the sky,
Through fluffy clouds, so fast we fly!

One day, we'll find a hidden land,
With castles tall and beaches grand.
Until that time, he'll stay with me,
My dragon friend, so wild and free!

Joshua Francis (8)
Nunthorpe Primary Academy, Nunthorpe

King Of The Field

King of the field, majestic in the grass.
Gracefully dining on the land.
Charismatic character standing so grand.
Spirit-free like trees in the windy sky.
Nobel and strong jumping so high.
Gentle beast, a mythical sight galloping across the emerald fields with all its might.
Watching horses makes me full of happiness and pride inside.
And even more when I go for a ride!

Molly Woolams (8)
Nunthorpe Primary Academy, Nunthorpe

The Lovely Summer

Summer is a time,
To play with your friends.
The laughter and the fun,
Never ends.
Don't stay inside,
Go and have fun,
You will enjoy,
The lovely sun.

Ice cream sundaes,
What a yummy delight.
Swimming in the sea,
Oh, I just might.
Late-night sunset,
I just love.
Saying goodnight,
To the sun above.
I love summer!

Tilly Hill (9)
Nunthorpe Primary Academy, Nunthorpe

Bye-Bye Winter

The fox looks in the clear lake,
The rabbit plays with the delicate leaves.
The hedgehog picks some fragrant flowers,
The squirrel climbs a sturdy tree.

There goes the money into a lake,
Make a wish and a butterfly appears.
The air is fresh and clear,
Here comes spring and bye-bye winter.

Martha Rance (8)
Nunthorpe Primary Academy, Nunthorpe

Autumn

Autumn is one of my favourite seasons
I'll give you lots of reasons
Kicking leaves and picking conkers
Running around and going bonkers
Squirrels up in trees in the park
Hoping to see a hedgehog, when it's dark
Finally, it's Halloween, trick or treating
Looking mean.

Harrison Land (9)
Nunthorpe Primary Academy, Nunthorpe

Friends

Friends are special
Friends are there when you get low
Friends are there to make you grow
Friends are there to make you laugh
And smile and run a mile
Friends are there to hug you...
Also bug you!
Friends come and go
But...
Friends are everything!

Miya Wilcox (8)
Nunthorpe Primary Academy, Nunthorpe

Untitled

In the middle of the night
At the North Pole
Snow fell fast,
And it was so, so cold.
My singing reindeer can
Fly across the dark, dark sky
Above the colourful Northern lights.
They deliver toys to all the
Sleeping boys and girls.

Lucas Day (9)
Nunthorpe Primary Academy, Nunthorpe

The Lonely Penguin

The lonely penguin,
Set off on his iceberg
All on his own
Looking for land and
Somewhere solid to stand.
A friendly seal popped up to say hello.
"Don't you think it's going to snow?" he said
In a quiet voice.

Harry Grainger (8)
Nunthorpe Primary Academy, Nunthorpe

Will The Future...?

Will the future
Have robot dogs?
Will the future
Have flying cars?
Will the future
Have hover scooters?
Will the future
Be bright?

Whatever the future has,
As long as we have each other.

Kit Falcon Sanderson (9)
Nunthorpe Primary Academy, Nunthorpe

The Champion

Sleek and light
The flight flew right
Double eighteen
I heard the crowd scream

Twenty left
Double ten, I need
Will I succeed?

The crowd went wild
Twenty I hit, and that was it!

Jake Manning (9)
Nunthorpe Primary Academy, Nunthorpe

Nine Years Old

Fortnite, Rocket League, FIFA, I adore,
Squash, cricket and football,
The sports I explore,
School time, playtime,
Science, English, maths
Home time, tea time,
Relax in the bath!

Rory Baines (9)
Nunthorpe Primary Academy, Nunthorpe

The Weather

The day is dark and gloomy,
I am at home feeling moody,
If only it were summer,
My day would be so much fun-ner,
So today, I will dream,
I will dream of summer.

Willow Charlton (8)
Nunthorpe Primary Academy, Nunthorpe

Space

S tars twinkle bright,
P lanets orbit the sun,
A stronauts, brave and bold,
C omets race around the galaxy,
E arth, home to many.

Evan Rowcliffe (9)
Nunthorpe Primary Academy, Nunthorpe

Fantastic Football

A haiku

Football is the best,
You can score amazing goals,
You will shout hooray!

Alfie Boalch (8)
Nunthorpe Primary Academy, Nunthorpe

Animal Dreams

Tiny tiger dreams...
Of snow where it cuddles its mum
The caged panda dreams...
Of going back to the jungle to eat a lot of bamboo
Sea jellyfish dreams...
A jellyfish swimming in the sea
Be careful of it, because it can sting you
If you see one, swim away from it carefully
Hurt hamster dreams...
There's a hamster on the road
All the cars waiting for it
But one of the cars crashed into him
Then he heard a voice
It was Mum, she said, "Wake up!"
I thought it was just a bad dream.

Sofiia Sribna (9)
Penruddock Primary School, Penruddock

Animal Dreams

The panda dreams...
Of crunching down on a
Lovely chunk of fresh bamboo.

The caught crab dreams...
Of scuttling along a colourful
Coral reef and bathing in
Magma vents.

The eagle dreams...
Of flying over huge mountain
Ranges and ancient cliff
Edges.

The bear dreams...
Of chewing on a
Lovely stack of sweet
Berries.

I dream of a
Huge ocean with an
Island just for me.

Ted Ware (9)
Penruddock Primary School, Penruddock

Animal Dream

The koala dreams...
Of lots of green leaves
The biggest tree to sleep on.

The adorable fox dreams...
Of an endless forest of trees
Where wild animals run.

The goat dreams...
Of the greenest grass in the world
Beautiful fields to live on.

The brave bear dreams...
Infinite food in the forest
And comfortable burrow to sleep in.

Daniil Sribnyi (11)
Penruddock Primary School, Penruddock

Animal Dreams

The cute kitten dreams...
Of a river with lots of fish
And a bed as comfy as candy.
The speedy cheetah dreams...
Of chasing an antelope
And pouncing onto it.
The shadow panther dreams...
Of hiding in the jungle trees
And pouncing on his prey
With courage.

Bertie Williamson (8)
Penruddock Primary School, Penruddock

Animal Dreams

A horse dreams
Of galloping across a field of beautiful silk grass
Set free cantering, jumping as many jumps as he wants
Then in the stable rolling in shavings
Eating the hay calmly.

Etta Goodall (8)
Penruddock Primary School, Penruddock

Dream

D ream of magic
R un up to the sky
E eek! The squeeze of a bitter lemon
A beautiful flowing stream
M agic falls into the sea.

Faith Fry (9)
Penruddock Primary School, Penruddock

Animal Dreams

The elephant dreams
Of eating leaves and carrots

Monkeys dream
Of causing mischief

Dogs dream
Of chasing rabbits.

Katie Kavanagh (9)
Penruddock Primary School, Penruddock

Another World

This was going to be an adventure of a lifetime.
I was tired of school.
Of everything. This world.
So, I'll just go to a different one, I thought.
I open my closet and think of a world of nature, a world of magic, a world of freedom.
I step through, everything fades.
I couldn't breathe, but I ran. I'm underwater.
I think of anything,
everything that can help me.
A school of fish and dolphins came from below,
pulling me up.
Fresh air blows against my face,
jungles, mountains, lakes, everything in a paradise.
I look up in relief and see birds,
dragons, phoenixes, islands... in the sky?
Name it, it's there.
This was going to be an adventure of a lifetime.

Natalie Harmas (11)
Sir Frederick Gibberd College, Harlow

Deep In The Jungle

D azzling,
E xtraordinary,
E mperor penguin,
P erforms like a brave orca.

I gloo survives snowstorms like a brave wolf.
N arwhal fights off orca like a soldier.

T he Amazon Rainforest has animals as fast as a car.
H ammerhead sharks are as weird as a blobfish!
E lks make deer as small as a guinea pig.

J aguars are as fierce as tigers.
U guisu is a type of bird that is as small as a mouse.
N ewts are as slimy as stingrays.
G orillas are as jacked as bodybuilders.
L lamas are as tall as a skyscraper.
E els are as disgusting as flies.

Jude Bain (10)
Stoneywood Primary School, Stoneywood

Scotland

S cotland oh how beautiful, just like a flower
C roft filled with heather and hay
O ceans as blue as the sky
T raditional tartan, your colours are beautiful
L and is so beautiful and gorgeous
A haggis for Robert Burns
N eeps to go with my haggis, oh how good
D ay will come when I will have to say goodbye.

Holly Mackenzie (10)
Stoneywood Primary School, Stoneywood

Untitled

Welcome reader to a wonderful story.

One morning, a girl woke up in a cabin which was her parents' home. She really liked it at the cabin, but one day the family was gone. It was really scary, but the next day, lots of birds came in the home and they partied all night.

One day, the birds were bored, so they went outside and played.

Happy ever after.

Nikola Kopilova (10)
Stoneywood Primary School, Stoneywood

Best Friends To The End

Everyone has a best friend
That they play with every day.
Everyone has a best friend
That they love in every way.

Whenever you are feeling sad,
Your best friend will find you and make you happy.
Our names are Maggie and Aggie
And we are very dappy.

Amelia Murray (10)
Stoneywood Primary School, Stoneywood

Friendship

A cord,
Oh a cord,
Of everlasting string,
Keeps me bound to my friend.
Even if,
You are countries afar,
This bond still,
Connects our hearts.
An unbreakable bond,
Impossible to sever,
Unless, alas,
Comes a bad thing.

Archer Hippey
Stoneywood Primary School, Stoneywood

Halloween Fright

Be careful on one scary night,
When lights go down,
It'll give you a fright,
The costumes, sweets and decorations,
The spooky night is such a fright,
A nice tradition for the young,
It's a fun party, so come along.

Daniel Oluwabusola (10)
Stoneywood Primary School, Stoneywood

The Blue Ocean

The blue ocean is clear as a crystal.
The ocean is warm and tropical, as if you can imagine.
The ocean is as bright as the sun.
It is quiet as a library.
It's calm but rapid as the world.

Fatima Imran (10)
Stoneywood Primary School, Stoneywood

Friends Forever

Through every up and every down,
We will stick together with a crown.
Through the smiles and frowns,
Us together is a crown.

Aimee-Louise Edgar (10)
Stoneywood Primary School, Stoneywood

Fluffy Clouds

F ields, fence, fire to blow out and behind them, cloud where the moon is about.
L adybird and butterflies flying high above the bright blue sky.
U mbrellas protect you from the rain when the clouds appear themselves again.
F eeling sad is a bad way to start your day.
F lying up high to wish the stars goodnight.
Y ou won't see the morning light when the beautiful bright stars appear at night.

C louds disappear to brighten my day.
L ove the feeling when the pretty sunshine comes out to shine!
O ur lives wouldn't be better without the clouds.
U mbrellas aren't for looking at, they are for using.
D ust is for wiping away, mud is for jumping in and love is not for breaking like stars.
S tars are pretty just like you!

Aubree Hutchinson (10)
Wise Esh Winning Academy, Esh Winning

The Man With The Ruby-Red Eyes

He stood over me with a glint in his eyes,
Forcefully warned me that I had to stay alive,
I was keen to fulfil this horrid journey,
Because it would allow me to thrive,
If I don't he will hit me with a sarcastic cry in his vermillion, ruby-red eyes,
I don't believe any of these silly little lies,
But I will have to if it will save my life,
The light blue in his tie really shocked my empty eyes,
I really need to take action,
I can't leave him with this passion,
If I leave him he could start bashing although he might start lashing,
It's really not glamorous, but I do need to start dashing!

Alarna Thompson (10)
Wise Esh Winning Academy, Esh Winning

Mission Gone Wrong

The rocket rammed into the moon and out came the mighty man
Among the clusters of dust
Then, as quick as a flash, he found out he was on the wrong planet
But his rocket was broken and so was his phone, so he couldn't call home
Then he wandered alone, bound to be up there forever
But a glint of hope, the ISS soared above
Then, he flew like a little dove
Trying to get to the hull
When he got through, he ran like a bull
He went to the phone to call all the way home
But home was all alone
So, he was stuck with nothing but a phone to keep him from being alone.

Logan Peart (11)
Wise Esh Winning Academy, Esh Winning

Seasons

Spring is green and pastel,
Filled with bunnies and lambs galore.
It is clean and Easter on the mantle,
Leaving out carrots for bunnies to gnaw.

Summer is yellow and bright,
Birds taking flight.
The buds are open,
And going to the sea with fellow friends.

Autumn is orange and cold,
Hedgehogs trot around the forest.
A mix of gold and mould,
Branches tied in a knot.

Winter is blue and white,
Bears hiding for the night.
Snow like glue builds,
Taking a stroll in it too.

Ivy Hodgson (11)
Wise Esh Winning Academy, Esh Winning

The Night Sky

The night is special, just like gold,
So, let's embrace the moment.
The stars are luminous and bold,
While the moon is taking its enrollment.

The empty sky is as dark as coal,
It's a beautifully painted picture.
So let us set our eyes,
On this glamorous picture.

The stars are perfectly aligned,
They're as bright as your personality.
It is better to look above you,
Than to face a sudden fatality.

Elsa-Mae Makepeace (10)
Wise Esh Winning Academy, Esh Winning

The Space World

Space is cool, just like Earth,
Rocks tumbling around the universe.

The night is timeless, just like space,
Shooting stars, flying with grace.

The sun is shining off the moon's face,
Rockets going from place to place.

Stars surrounding the Earth's flat face,
Comet by comet, starts a new place.

Making you think of such a wonderful place,
Gravity pulls, light rays shining bright like a glaze.

Logan Emmerson (11)
Wise Esh Winning Academy, Esh Winning

Large Pizza With Red Sausage!

Roses are red
Pizza sauce is too
I ordered a large
It was for me
But I might share it with you
It was pepperoni
It wasn't very nice
Because it also had a hint of mice
Violets are blue
Chickens are nice
Please don't ask
Because I also have lice
I like the Spice Girls
They are the best
They are my favourite
Because they have their own vest
So I like a lot of things!

Jacob Jobson (10)
Wise Esh Winning Academy, Esh Winning

Capybaras

C urious creatures basking in the sun.
A mbling by the water where their life began.
P layful splashes in the river.
Y awning in the evening under the stars so bright.
B eneath the water, they played.
A fter food, they sleep through the night.
R elaxed and plump they take their time.
A riverbank full of them.
S unny days are best for their big naps.

Jay Bragan (11)
Wise Esh Winning Academy, Esh Winning

A Paca's Journey

In a different world, life flourished
Little animals called pacas roamed this land
Happily grazing on fresh grass
But the little pacas had to get new grass to graze on
So they travelled and travelled across hilly mountains and dark woods
When they arrived at the meadow, they grazed on more grass
Then they set off again, back through the hilly mountains and the dark woods.

Oliver James (11)
Wise Esh Winning Academy, Esh Winning

Larry With His Friend, Barry!

Hi, my name is Larry and I have thirty kids.
I love going fishing and that is it.
I also do the dishes. They are a mess.
I also like playing Dress To Impress.
I have a friend. He is called Barry, but we call him Bahh.
I like trees. They are the best
And I only say yes.
Don't be stupid or you might become a mess.

Raegan Arrowsmith (11)
Wise Esh Winning Academy, Esh Winning

Fancy

F ancy things are more posh than other things.
A nyone you are, you're still fancy for everything you have.
N othing is more posh than you.
C an you see the light when you wear something fancy?
Y ou're still fancy or posh when you want to be.

Lillie Davy (10)
Wise Esh Winning Academy, Esh Winning

Hamster

H iding in my pocket
A ll they are thinking about is food, all day
M aster escape artists
S hredding carrots all day
T iny paws capable of climbing
E agerly exploring with a fearless heart
R acing wheels that spin and twirl.

Ella-Jane Walker (11)
Wise Esh Winning Academy, Esh Winning

The Dragon's Cave

Near the dragon's cave,
The sky filled with shimmer,
Fires burn bright, so it would glimmer,
The dragon sleeps, breathing out air,
The last thing I want is to share.
The dragon's cave is really quiet.
With leaves scattered all around it.

Lexi Leigh Kirby (11)
Wise Esh Winning Academy, Esh Winning

Food And Lice

I love food,
So do you.
I wonder if you can smell it, too?
I ordered some,
It didn't come nice
I think it had a hint of lice.

I chucked it away
(Or maybe I didn't)
So I ordered food
(Totally without lice!)

Sofia Graham (10)
Wise Esh Winning Academy, Esh Winning

Space World

S pace was wonderful, like an Atlantic city
P lanets were colourful, like a rainbow
A s spectacular as Earth
C ity was bouncing as we landed on beautiful Earth
E arth was in danger from a bright, burning meteor.

Jack McAngus (11)
Wise Esh Winning Academy, Esh Winning

Labrador

L oveable
A dorable
B right and beautiful
R un like the wind
A dventurous
D elightful
O pposite of calm
R eally crazy.

Olivia Wayper (11)
Wise Esh Winning Academy, Esh Winning

A Blue Miffkin

It is as small as a mouse
It is as blue as the Atlantic Ocean
It is as fast as a cheetah
It is as cute as a fairy
It is as good at hiding as a chameleon
It is a blue miffkin.

Skye Heath (10)
Wise Esh Winning Academy, Esh Winning

The Amazing Food

Food is amazing,
But so is saving,
I can't spend money,
But I can't stop craving,
It's not just food,
It's drinks too.
I ordered food,
But I might sue.

Jesse Brown (10)
Wise Esh Winning Academy, Esh Winning

Untitled

Trees fall on people so tall,
Bees buzz like a street hum,
Grass reaches for the sky,
In the night we will fly,
So long we will say
As we fly away,
Hooray!

Evie Kirkup (10)
Wise Esh Winning Academy, Esh Winning

Magic

Roses are red
Magic is blue
And I love glitter
Just like you

Glitter is nice
Glitter is cool
And I love glitter
Just like you.

Hollie Lyon (10)
Wise Esh Winning Academy, Esh Winning

Portal

P ortal
O ther dimension
R ift in time
T ime and space
A lternative world
L eaning universe.

Lucas Hodgson (11)
Wise Esh Winning Academy, Esh Winning

Space

S tars everywhere
P lanets circling
A liens destroying planets
C omets crashing
E arth needing safety.

Teddy Peveller (10)
Wise Esh Winning Academy, Esh Winning

YOUNG WRITERS INFORMATION

We hope you have enjoyed reading this book – and that you will continue to in the coming years.

If you're the parent or family member of an enthusiastic poet or story writer, do visit our website **www.youngwriters.co.uk/subscribe** and sign up to receive news, competitions, writing challenges and tips, activities and much, much more! There's lots to keep budding writers motivated!

If you would like to order further copies of this book, or any of our other titles, then please give us a call or order via your online account.

Young Writers
Remus House
Coltsfoot Drive
Peterborough
PE2 9BF
(01733) 890066
info@youngwriters.co.uk

Join in the conversation!
Tips, news, giveaways and much more!

- YoungWritersUK
- YoungWritersCW
- youngwriterscw
- youngwriterscw

Scan Me!